ASK US ABOUT US

A Campaign for Correct Representation

Come to Common Ground

by
RC "Majid" Woolen Jr.

Final Draft – October 2025

© 2025 RC "Majid" Woolen Jr. All Rights Reserved.

Library of Congress Cataloging -in-Publication Data

ISBN 979-8-218-94342-4

Published in the United States by

Majid Enterprises, Inc.

3540 E. Broad St. 120-408 Mansfield, TX 76063-5633

Phone: 1-888-99-MAJID (6-2543)

info@majidenterprisesinc.com

www.majidenterprisesinc.com

FOREWORD

FOREWORD

I come to believe that a nation, much like a man, must rise from within before it can stand before the world. Strength does not come from noise, nor healing from denial. Both the man and the nation must confront their own reflection, admit their errors, and remember the principles that once made them whole.

I have lived long enough to see America lose its balance—not because its foundation failed, but because its moral compass began to spin. We have traded understanding for outrage, conscience for convenience, and leadership for performance. Yet I still believe in the heart of this nation, because I have seen it reflected in the people who rise every morning to work, raise children, and keep faith alive in quiet ways.

I did not come to politics through ambition. I came through observation—watching a nation of extraordinary people being misrepresented by ordinary selfishness. The more I watched, the clearer it became: what America needs is not another party savior but a moral awakening among its people. That is what this book is about. It is a campaign, yes—but not merely for votes. It is a campaign for correct representation, where honesty speaks louder than loyalty to any banner, and where faith, family, and freedom once again find their rightful place.

I write as a father of six children—each a reminder that the future is not an idea, but a face. I write as a man who has stumbled and stood, who has been bound down and risen again, who has learned that integrity is not inherited; it is chosen, every day. And I write as an American who refuses to surrender this country's soul to the loudest voices of division.

If I can convince even one reader to stand taller, listen deeper, and mend one torn piece of this national garment, then my effort will not be in vain. We cannot afford to keep living as if truth were optional and unity outdated. The time has come to stand again, to mend again, to believe again.

This is my offering to that cause. — RC "Majid" Woolen Jr.

TABLE OF CONTENTS

Ask Us About Us – RC "Majid" Woolen Jr.

Chapter 1 – Qiyam: Arise

Chapter 1 – Qiyam: Arise

Before you talk about us, ask us about us.

That simple phrase might sound like common sense, but in America today, common sense has become a rare language. Politicians, pundits, and platforms spend billions every year trying to define who *we* are — the people — without ever sitting down to listen. They build their campaigns around assumptions, not understanding. They design policies based on numbers, not neighbors.

Every election cycle, someone new claims to "speak for" the people. But when you listen close, they're really speaking *about* the people — talking around us like we're not in the room. They take polls, not conversations. They run analytics, not empathy.

I've come to understand that if you want to know a person, you look them in the eye and you ask. You don't decide for them, and you don't assume their story. You ask. I have grown to find that there is a power of transparency there at that time.

But somewhere along the way, America stopped asking.

Instead, we started labeling.

We started dividing people into neat little groups and folders — blue and red, liberal and conservative, black and white, believer and skeptic, rich and poor — and we told each group what they were supposed to believe.

7

Now, we live in a country where everyone's talking, but nobody's listening.

The Unheard Voices

There's a whole generation of Americans who don't fit cleanly into any of those boxes. Folks who grew up in neighborhoods where faith still matters but so does fairness. People who respect tradition but also understand change. People who want strong borders and open opportunity. People who believe in God and in good government.

We're told we're contradictions. We're told we have to pick a side. But the truth is, *we are the middle ground America forgot it had.*

You can find us in the church, in the mosque, in the barber shop, at the mechanic's, on the construction site, in the small business, or sitting at the kitchen table trying to figure out why the cost of living is rising faster than the paycheck. We're not extremists. We're not ideologues. We're everyday citizens who want what's right — not what's left or right.

And yet, both parties act like we don't exist.

The Democrats assume they already have us. The Republicans assume we don't matter.

Well, I'm here to say — "Ask Us About Us."

Because we're not anybody's property.

The Problem with Representation

Representation in America has turned into a business. Parties treat communities like territories, not people. If you look at it closely, politics has become more about control than care.

When politicians talk about "the Black vote," or "the Latino vote," or "the working-class vote," they're talking strategy, not service. They don't see individuals — they see demographics. They don't see your life — they see your data.

That's not representation. That's management.

And that's why I'm running — to challenge that system. Because America doesn't need managers; America needs messengers who understand both the language of the people and the responsibility of leadership.

You can't represent people you don't respect. You can't legislate for people you never listen to.

Between Two Worlds

I've lived long enough to see both sides of America — the promise and the pain, the light and the limitations.

I've seen the strength in one group and the struggle in another.

And I've watched how both have been told the other is the enemy.

But what I see is this: both sides have value. Both sides have something sacred to protect.

One has deep roots in tradition, in God, in country, in structure. The other has deep roots in compassion, in justice, in fighting for the underdog. What we've lost is the balance between the two — the center that used to hold this nation together.

I'm not with one side *against* the other. I'm standing between them, with my arms stretched out, trying to sew the two back together. Because if one side represents the left sleeve and the other the right, then America is the garment that's been ripped down the middle.

It's time to mend it.

Why I Refuse to Be Owned

For too long, the Democratic Party has assumed ownership over minority voices. The Republican Party has often spoken *at us*, not *with us*. I don't say that in anger — I say it as observation.

The Democratic Party's history with social programs has created dependency where there should have been development. The Republican Party's history with rhetoric has created division where there should have been dialogue.

Both have forgotten that the goal of leadership is not control — it's correction.

I don't belong to either. I belong to the truth. And if that truth makes me sound conservative one day and compassionate the next, that's fine — because that's what balance sounds like.

My campaign isn't against the Democratic Party or the Republican Party — it's against the dysfunction that's taken over both.

The New Conservative Voice

When I call myself a conservative, I mean something deeper than party politics.

I mean conserving what's good — our moral foundation, our sense of order, our duty to God and to one another — while also being open to progress that uplifts, not destroys.

I'm not afraid of new ideas. I'm afraid of losing old truths.

Because without truth, progress is chaos dressed up in a nice suit.

Conservative doesn't mean closed-minded — it means clear-minded. It means we preserve what's sacred so we can build what's necessary.

That's the kind of conservatism I stand for: one that doesn't shout, but serves; one that doesn't divide, but defends; one that doesn't look down on people, but looks out for them.

Listening Is Leadership

If we want a stronger Congress, we have to rebuild communication.

Politics today is like two people arguing in a room with no windows — everyone's yelling, but nobody's breathing.

The foundation of leadership is listening. And not listening to respond — listening to *understand*.

That's what I want to bring to Washington — a spirit of Qiyam, a standing up from being bound down by old systems, party expectations, and social stereotypes. Because America doesn't need another echo chamber. It needs ears.

Ask. Don't Assume.

Ask Us About Us – RC "Majid" Woolen Jr.

Before you write your next headline, your next law, your next speech — *Ask Us.*

Ask the mother who works two jobs why she still believes in faith.

Ask the young man in the city why he's skeptical of both parties.

Ask the family running a small business why taxes are choking their dreams.

Ask the child why they stopped believing in their country.

Ask them.

Because the answers you'll hear are not about just race or party — they're about being human.

When I say "Ask Us About Us," I'm not just talking to politicians — I'm talking to all of us.

To media, to educators, to voters, to leaders, to parents, to pastors, to neighbors.

We can't fix what we refuse to face. And we can't face what we won't ask about.

So, this chapter — this message — is my invitation: let's start the asking again.

Because when we stop assuming and start asking, that's when America begins to heal.

Before a man can rise, he must recognize what has kept him bound down. Awakening begins not with anger, but awareness

Ask Us About Us – RC "Majid" Woolen Jr.

— the moment a man stands and refuses to stay tied to the past.
America, too, must stand again, not in rebellion, but in renewal.

— • —

Chapter 2 The Garment of America

Chapter 2 – The Garment of America

America is a beautiful garment — stitched together from threads of every color, pattern, and history. Yet today, that garment is torn. It's been pulled apart by fear, mistrust, and misunderstanding. You can see the frayed edges in our politics, in our neighborhoods, even in our homes.

But the good news is this: what has been torn *can be mended*.

And mending begins with honesty.

Before you label me, hear me.

I am African American — raised by strength, by history, by endurance.

I am Native American — rooted in the soil of this land, carrying the spirit of those who walked it first.

I am a Muslim American — guided by faith, discipline, and peace.

But above all that, I am an American.

That's the common ground I stand on — the ground we all share.

So let's meet there. Let's do what's best for America.

The Rip and the Thread

When a piece of clothing tears, most people throw it away. They figure it's cheaper to replace than to repair. That's what we've been doing as a country — throwing away people, principles, and traditions instead of stitching them back together.

We've thrown away conversation.

We've thrown away forgiveness.

We've thrown away the art of listening.

But a good tailor knows that when a fabric rips, the best thing you can do is find a strong thread and begin to sew. That thread must be both flexible and firm. That's what truth is — flexible enough to meet people where they are, firm enough not to break under pressure.

Our job, as Americans, is to be that thread. To be part of the repair.

The Role of Communication

Most of our problems aren't about laws — they're about listening. We're arguing about symptoms while ignoring the silence beneath them.

You can't sew if you won't touch the fabric. You can't heal if you won't face the wound.

Communication is contact. It's sitting down with people who see the world differently and saying, "Let's find the part of this we can fix together." That's what our Congress was designed to do — deliberate, not dominate.

That's why I say I'm running to strengthen Congress — because it's supposed to be the sewing room of democracy. That's where ideas are cut, measured, hemmed, and joined. When that room breaks down, the whole garment comes apart.

The Danger of Division

We've allowed politics to divide us the way scissors divide cloth. We slice through relationships, communities, even families. We call it "progress," but most of the time it's pride.

Every movement — conservative, liberal, progressive, or populist — carries pieces of truth. But truth doesn't live inside a party; it lives in the courage to face the whole picture.

That's why I refuse to speak in hatred of either side. Because hate is acid — it eats the thread, weakens the fabric, and leaves the garment thinner than before.

If one side insists on tearing and the other insists on cutting, who will be left to sew?

We the People, the Weavers

Ask Us About Us – RC "Majid" Woolen Jr.

The Founders of this nation weren't perfect, but they were builders. They took 13 very different colonies and wove them into a single cloth. Over time, more threads were added — through struggle, through sacrifice, through amendment and reform. Each generation patched something, fixed something, or added a new design.

Now, it's our turn.

Our generation's test is not whether we can fight, but whether we can *fix*.

Whether we can respect the pattern of our history while sewing a stronger, fairer fabric for our children.

We have to be the weavers again — in politics, in neighborhoods, in faith communities, in classrooms.

That's how we make America durable again.

My Thread in the Cloth

Being African American taught me endurance.

Being Native American taught me respect for the land and the people who came before me.

Being Muslim American taught me discipline, patience, and purpose.

Being simply American taught me that unity is not uniformity —
it's harmony.

Each part of me represents a thread — distinct, but connected.
And together, they make something that no single strand could
make alone.

That's how I see America.

Not a melting pot where everything loses flavor, but a fabric
where every thread keeps its color and still serves the whole.

The Work of Repair

Repair doesn't happen by accident. It takes time, tools, and
intention.

It means acknowledging where we've been wrong without
abandoning where we've been right. It means holding
accountability without losing compassion. It means standing up
— Qiyam — to lift this nation back to its higher self.

And it starts small.

A handshake instead of a hashtag.

A conversation instead of a comment thread.

A neighborly act instead of a political argument.

That's how the garment starts to come back together — one stitch, one truth, one person at a time.

The Call to Common Ground

So, before we tear another seam, before we walk away from one another again, let's remember what's written at the top of our nation's fabric: E Pluribus Unum — "Out of many, one."

It doesn't say "Out of one, a few." It says *out of many.*

That means our differences are not defects — they're design.

If we can accept that, then we can start building again.

If we can respect that, then we can start healing again.

And if we can live that, then maybe, just maybe, the garment of America can shine again — whole, strong, and worthy of the people who wear it.

Closing Reflection

I'm not running to replace old fabric with new — I'm running to repair the one that still fits.

I'm not asking America to become something different — I'm asking her to remember what she was meant to be.

Because at the end of the day, no matter our color, faith, or politics — we are threads of the same flag, citizens of the same country, and children of the same promise.

And the time to mend is now.

A nation torn is like a garment ripped by careless hands. Mending it takes patience, not pride. If we can stitch our faith, our freedom, and our families back together — thread by thread — we can wear unity again with dignity.

— • —

Chapter 3 Between Two Parties

Chapter 3 – Between Two Parties

America stands at a crossroads — not of maps, but of minds.

The left and the right glare at one another across a divide so deep that even truth seems to echo differently on each side.
Somewhere in between that shouting match, ordinary people are trying to live, raise their children, pay their bills, and make sense of a country that feels divided by design.

I don't stand with one side just because history or tradition says I should. I don't lean left because my community expects it. I don't bow right because of my faith or my conservatism. I stand between two parties — not because I can't decide, but because I've already decided: my loyalty belongs to what's right, not who's right.

There was a time when both parties carried meaning beyond slogans.

The Democratic Party once spoke of the working man — the one whose hands built America's bridges, schools, and streets. It claimed to defend the poor and lift up the marginalized. But over time, that same voice became tangled in bureaucracy and dependency. It created programs that helped in the short term but hurt in the long run, turning empowerment into entitlement. It started to speak *for* people instead of *with* them.

Now, when I listen to much of the modern Democratic message, I don't hear freedom; I hear control. I hear a party that wants to fix what it helped to break, using the same tools that caused the damage. It preaches compassion but practices confusion — especially when it comes to culture, faith, and family.

Ask Us About Us – RC "Majid" Woolen Jr.

I have seen communities encouraged to depend on government handouts instead of being inspired to build their own independence. I have seen leaders promise opportunity while quietly keeping the gates locked. I cannot, in good conscience, be consumed by a machine that profits from my vote but rarely respects my voice.

And yet, I also cannot ignore the other side of the aisle — the Republican Party.

I have conservative values. I believe in responsibility, faith, family, and the strength that comes from discipline. But too often, what I see from the modern Republican establishment doesn't reflect the heart of conservatism; it reflects the pride of elitism. It's not about stewardship — it's about status. It's not about moral clarity — it's about moral superiority.

There are good conservatives who still believe in true freedom — the kind that uplifts, not oppresses — but they are often drowned out by the louder voices of arrogance and entitlement. I have felt that *"I am better than he"* attitude that seeps into policy debates, community outreach, and even personal interaction. It's as though compassion became weakness and understanding became compromise.

In Texas, I see both sides playing tug-of-war over the same people — families, small business owners, educators, churchgoers — each claiming to represent their interests, while neither really listens. The Democratic side promises help but demands loyalty. The Republican side preaches freedom but guards privilege. And in between them stands the rest of us, watching America's garment stretch thinner with every election cycle.

That's why I believe the future isn't blue or red — it's *correct*.

Correct representation means we no longer settle for being managed by parties that treat us like markets instead of citizens. It means leadership that understands a parent's desire to guide their child's future, not have it dictated by ideology. It means respecting faith without forcing religion, and embracing equality without erasing difference.

Standing between two parties isn't confusion — it's clarity. It's the moment of Qiyam — rising from the bondage of expectation and standing in truth.

Independence isn't rebellion; it's responsibility. It's the ability to think beyond slogans and act beyond fear.

I've learned that America doesn't need more political soldiers — it needs bridge builders. People who can look both ways and see value on each side. People who understand that progress isn't about moving left or right — it's about moving forward, together.

When I talk about strengthening Congress, I don't mean packing it with more politicians. I mean filling it with people who still remember why the seats were built — to serve. To listen. To work. Not to perform. Not to divide.

The role of a representative is not to echo a party line, but to carry the people's truth into policy. That truth doesn't come from a platform; it comes from prayer, conversation, and conscience.

Ask Us About Us – RC "Majid" Woolen Jr.

Correct representation means I see you — not your label, not your income, not your vote. Just you.

It means I will fight for what is *right*, not what is *popular*. Because popularity fades, but principle endures.

The Democrats need humility. The Republicans need empathy. And America needs both.

It's time to stop choosing sides and start choosing standards.

It's time to stop chasing colors and start chasing character.

It's time to mend the torn garment of America, thread by thread — with patience, wisdom, and care.

That's what it means to stand between two parties.

Not lost. Not undecided.

But risen — bound down no longer.

Parties are just names — purpose is eternal. The donkey and the elephant have both carried America forward and sometimes led her astray. But the true strength of this land rests not in the party we serve, but in the principles we protect.

— • —

Chapter 4 The Children and the Future

Chapter 4 – The Children and the Future

Every generation believes it loves its children. But not every generation protects them.

Some love them in sentiment, but not in structure. Some praise them on television while poisoning the world they'll inherit. The true measure of a nation isn't in its military, its markets, or even its monuments — it's in how it shapes the minds of its youth and guards the innocence of its children.

Our children are not political projects. They are not experiments. They are human beings created with a natural identity, a natural curiosity, and a natural desire to learn.

Some things in life are meant to be discovered — not decided by committee.

I believe a child's understanding of who they are should grow in time, through nurture, conversation, and truth — not through confusion, pressure, or political agendas. Nature doesn't rush. It unfolds. We should allow children to unfold too.

There are voices today trying to turn childhood into a battlefield — where innocence is mistaken for ignorance and guidance is replaced with ideology. That isn't progress; it's manipulation. We should never allow the next generation to be sacrificed for the sake of adult debates.

When I speak about protecting our children, I don't speak out of fear — I speak out of faith. Faith in the Creator who designed life with wisdom. Faith in the natural order that guides growth, one honest step at a time. Faith in the truth that we are guardians of something precious, not owners of something disposable.

The family is the first school, and the home is the first classroom. Long before a teacher explains a lesson, a parent has already written one in the heart of a child. That's why family policy must be national priority — not a talking point. We can't strengthen schools while weakening the household. We can't expect educators to teach what parents no longer live.

In Texas, debates about school funding and vouchers are growing louder. Some see them as a doorway to opportunity; others see them as a threat to public education. I believe they can be a bridge — if we use them wisely. Vouchers should empower parents to choose what's best for their child, not abandon public schools to fail. Charter schools and private institutions can innovate and lead, but they must also uplift the same communities public education was created to serve.

Education, at its best, should not only prepare a student to earn a living — it should prepare them to live honorably.

We've spent decades teaching children how to make money, but too little time teaching them what to make of themselves.

Discipline. Integrity. Respect. These are not outdated values — they are survival tools for a free society.

A new education system must include the heart and the mind. Science and spirit. Numbers and names. The power of technology should never outgrow the power of morality.

Ask Us About Us – RC "Majid" Woolen Jr.

The danger of the current path is clear: when identity becomes political and truth becomes optional, children lose their compass. A society without a moral compass doesn't lose its direction overnight — it drifts, quietly, until it no longer recognizes the shore.

Our duty — as parents, educators, lawmakers, and neighbors — is to restore that compass. To remind our children that freedom is not the right to do anything; it's the strength to do the right thing.

The Congress I wish to strengthen should reflect that responsibility. We should fight less over who gets the credit and more over how we build the future. We must protect the spaces where our children grow — their schools, their homes, their communities — from confusion, corruption, and neglect.

The goal is not to control what they think, but to teach them *how* to think — clearly, kindly, and courageously. To help them see that identity is not something granted by government, but something grown within the human soul.

We are shaping tomorrow's leaders right now. Every policy passed, every budget signed, every lesson taught in a classroom writes a chapter in the story of a child's life. If that story begins with division and fear, then the future will echo the same.

But if it begins with clarity, compassion, and conviction, then America will have raised a generation that no longer sees color as competition, or difference as danger — but character as destiny.

Children don't just inherit our nation; they inherit our example.

And if we do right by them — if we protect their right to be children and guide their path toward wisdom — then maybe, just maybe, they will look back one day and say that we were the generation who stopped arguing long enough to build something that lasted.

Because the future isn't something we wait for —

it's someone we raise.

— • —

Chapter 5 Faith, Freedom, and Responsibility

Chapter 5 – Faith, Freedom, and Responsibility

Freedom without faith is fragile.

And faith without responsibility is hollow.

The two are bound together — not by law, but by purpose. One gives us the right to choose; the other teaches us how to choose rightly.

America was built upon the belief that human beings are endowed by a Creator with rights that no man can take away. That idea isn't political, it's, spiritual. It's what separates liberty from chaos and democracy from decay. Yet somewhere along the line, we began to worship freedom while forgetting its source.

We've turned the word "freedom" into a slogan, something to shout at rallies or post online. But freedom is not noise — it's a noble silence that lets conscience speak. It's a sacred trust that must be handled with care.

True freedom doesn't mean doing whatever we please; it means doing what's right even when no one is watching.

It's the understanding that responsibility is not the enemy of liberty — it's its guardian.

Faith gives freedom its direction. Without faith, freedom can lose its moral compass and drift into indulgence, corruption, and confusion. Faith reminds us that life has meaning beyond pleasure, that truth is not up for vote, and that duty is not optional.

Ask Us About Us – RC "Majid" Woolen Jr.

I've seen what happens when faith is removed from public life
— when morality is treated like a private hobby instead of a
public virtue. Society begins to unravel, not because people
become less intelligent, but because they become less
accountable. You can't legislate conscience, but you can
encourage it.

That's the role of leadership — not to enforce belief, but to
preserve the soil where belief can grow.

When Congress debates policy, it often does so as if faith and
government must stand on opposite sides of a wall. I see it
differently. Faith is not meant to rule over law — it's meant to
inform it. It gives moral meaning to freedom and human depth to
democracy.

When a lawmaker takes an oath, it's not just to a constitution
written on paper — it's to a truth written on the heart. That truth
whispers that power is borrowed, not owned; that authority is
service, not status.

Faith teaches humility, and humility is the cornerstone of just
leadership. A leader who forgets to kneel before something
greater than himself will eventually bow before his own ego.

We must bring faith back into the conversation — not as
doctrine, but as direction. Because a nation that loses its
reverence will soon lose its restraint.

In Texas, I've met people from every walk of life —
churchgoers, small business owners, immigrants, farmers,
teachers. They may differ in denomination, race, or culture, but

nearly all agree on one thing: America works best when people believe in something higher than themselves. That belief is what holds the line between liberty and lawlessness.

Responsibility begins with the individual. It means showing up, following through, telling the truth, paying what you owe, and teaching your children to do the same. It's not glamorous, but it's greatness in its purest form.

We often demand accountability from our government, but the government is a reflection of us. If the people are careless, the laws will be weak. If the citizens are selfish, the system will be corrupt. The strength of a republic is not in the marble of its buildings but in the morality of its people.

That's why freedom must always walk hand in hand with responsibility. You can't have one without the other and still call it justice.

To be truly free is to be answerable — not just to the law, but to your conscience. To your Creator. To your community. To your children who are watching what you choose today and will live with the consequences tomorrow.

The day faith leaves the heart of a nation, the lights start to dim — not all at once, but one by one. Hope grows cold, division grows loud, and truth becomes negotiable. But it doesn't have to stay that way. We can still rise — still remember — still rebuild.

Faith, freedom, and responsibility are not old ideas. They are eternal ones.

And when we return to them, not out of fear but out of conviction, we'll find that America's strength was never in its parties, its power, or its politics — it was always in its principles.

Those principles begin in the soul of every citizen, in the still moment when one asks not, "What can I get?" but "What can I give?"

That is the question that renews a nation.

That is the heartbeat of correct representation.

And that is the kind of Congress I seek to strengthen — one guided not just by rules, but by reverence.

— • —

Chapter 6 The Garment and the Gap

Chapter 6 – The Garment and the Gap

America was stitched together with vision, not perfection.

Our founders wove a garment meant to cover generations — a cloth of liberty, justice, and opportunity for all who would wear it. They knew it would fray in places. They knew it would need mending. But they believed it was worth the work.

Today, that garment is showing its age. The seams are strained by anger, mistrust, and division. Threads that once bound us together — respect, faith, family, and community — are being pulled apart by politics and pride. We can feel the gaps between us widening. But what's most dangerous is not that the cloth is torn; it's that too many have stopped trying to mend it.

The garment is America itself.

And the gap — that's us.

We've become accustomed to pointing fingers instead of threading needles. We blame rather than bind. We argue over who caused the tear instead of asking who will repair it.

But I've learned something: a nation doesn't heal through accusation. It heals through attention. Through care. Through the courage to sit down, side by side, and sew.

Every generation inherits the garment of its country. Some receive it clean and crisp; others, tattered and stained by the struggles of the past. Ours is both — proud and worn, beautiful and burdened. It tells a story of triumph and trauma, progress and pain.

And that's alright. Because the worth of the garment isn't in its condition — it's in our commitment to restore it.

When we see a rip, we have two choices:

We can pull it wider to prove our point, or we can pick up the thread and repair what remains.

Repair doesn't mean pretending the tear isn't there. It means acknowledging it — studying its edges — understanding why it formed. Maybe the fabric was stretched too thin. Maybe the tension went unchecked. Maybe we simply forgot to care for what we inherited. Whatever the reason, mending requires patience, precision, and love.

If you keep pulling at the hole, you'll have nothing left to patch. That's what's happening to our nation. We keep pulling — over race, over religion, over class, over politics — and we forget that the strength of America is not in the sameness of its fabric, but in the stitching that holds its differences together.

To mend the garment, we must first respect the thread.

The thread is our shared humanity — the belief that every person, no matter their origin or opinion, has value. It's the thread of faith that reminds us we are accountable to something greater than ourselves. It's the thread of duty that tells us freedom is not free, that the cloth survives only if each of us tends to our corner.

Ask Us About Us – RC "Majid" Woolen Jr.

I've seen too many people give up on the idea of unity. They
say, "America's too divided now." But I disagree. Division isn't
new — it's just louder. We've argued since our beginning, but
we've also rebuilt again and again. The Civil War didn't end the
dream, the Civil Rights Movement didn't destroy the fabric, they
strengthened it. Each struggle made the garment tougher, more
honest, more inclusive.

The question now is not whether America can be mended. It's
whether we still believe it's worth mending.

It starts small. A conversation instead of a confrontation. A
handshake instead of a headline. Listening more than labeling.
That's how you sew a torn nation — one stitch at a time.

And Texas, with its diversity and bold spirit, can lead that
example. We are a living patchwork — cities and countrysides,
oil fields and tech hubs, Black, White, Latino, Asian, and Native
— all bound by one promise we are Texans, and we are
Americans.

If we can mend here, we can mend anywhere.

It's time we pick up the needle again — not as Democrats or
Republicans, but as neighbors, parents, workers, and believers.
The garment doesn't need a perfect tailor, it needs willing hands.

Because the truth is, no matter how many tears it gets, this fabric
of ours is still strong. It's been tested by centuries and never
fully torn apart.

Ask Us About Us – RC "Majid" Woolen Jr.

We just need to remember how to thread the needle — with
humility, hope, and hard work.

And when we do, we'll find that the gaps between us are not as
wide as we thought. They're waiting for us to close them, not
with words, but with action.

Let us be the generation that refuses to pull at the holes and
instead patches the promise. Let us mend America, stitch by
stitch, until once again, it becomes what it was always meant to
be — one nation, woven together by faith, bound down only by
the laws of decency and duty, and lifted up by the strength of our
shared humanity.

— • —

Chapter 7 The Mirror and the Mandate

Chapter 7 – The Mirror and the Mandate

Every nation must face itself.

Not in moments of triumph, but in moments of trial. It is in those times, when the noise of blame fades and the dust of division settles, that we find ourselves standing before the mirror.

What we see staring back is not the government. It is not the President, the Congress, or the courts. It's us — *the people*. The reflection belongs to every one of us.

The mirror never lies. It doesn't flatter or excuse. It shows the truth of who we are and what we've allowed. And what it shows America now is uncomfortable — but necessary.

We've grown accustomed to criticizing leaders for their failures, and many times we're right to do so. Corruption, greed, and cowardice have crept into places where courage and conviction once stood. Too many representatives have forgotten that their title is not a throne — it's a trust.

But as citizens, we cannot escape our own reflection either. Leadership doesn't appear in a vacuum. It rises from among us. The leaders we get are a mirror of the people who send them. If we demand entertainment over integrity, we'll get performers instead of policymakers. If we prize anger over understanding, we'll get outrage instead of outcomes.

The mirror cuts both ways.

That's why the mandate — the authority of the people — must be earned and exercised with wisdom. We cannot continue to send the same type of people to Congress and expect a different kind of government. We cannot continue to reward division and expect unity.

I'm running to strengthen Congress — not to simply occupy a seat, but to remind the institution of its original purpose: representation rooted in responsibility. A Congress that reflects the courage of its people, not the corruption of its donors. A Congress that debates fiercely but governs faithfully.

But this chapter of our history demands something from citizens, too.

Democracy is not a spectator sport — *and believe me they are trying to sideline us* — It's a covenant, a living promise between the governed and those who govern. If we break it from either side, the whole structure begins to rot.

We must return to civic honesty — that clear-eyed willingness to admit when we've gone astray, and to correct course without shame. We must teach our children that freedom is not a handout from the powerful, but a duty entrusted to the humble.

When we stand before the mirror, we must ask hard questions:

Have we demanded truth, or just comfort?

Have we held our leaders accountable, or have we excused them because they sound like us?

Have we listened to understand, or only to reply?

A people that avoids reflection invites ruin.

In Texas, where I live and hope to serve, that reflection runs deep. Texans take pride in independence, but true independence comes with responsibility. We don't just talk about liberty; we live it. But liberty without discipline is chaos. Freedom without faith becomes self-interest. And power without principle becomes tyranny, no matter who holds it.

The mandate of the people is sacred. It is not a blank check — it's a loan of trust. Every two, four, or six years, we decide whether to renew that loan. But that decision is only as wise as the honesty we bring to the mirror.

And so, as I prepare to serve, I look in that mirror too.

I don't see perfection. I see a man still learning, still growing, still bound down at times by the limits of his own experience. But I also see a man willing to stand up, to rise, to mend what he can, and to tell the truth even when it's unpopular.

That's the kind of reflection I believe our nation needs more of — not flawless leaders, but faithful ones. Not people who act like they have all the answers, but people who aren't afraid to ask the right questions.

Because at the end of the day, when the speeches are over and the elections are done, the mirror will still be there. It will still be asking us, *"who are we?"*.

And the mandate, that precious trust between citizen and representative, will depend on how honestly we answer.

The strength of a nation doesn't come from the mirror being clean — it comes from the courage to face it.

And when we finally do, we'll realize something powerful: the reflection was never our enemy. It was our reminder.

— • —

Chapter 8 – Children of the Crossroads

Chapter 8 – Children of the Crossroads

Guiding the Next Generation Through a Divided America

Every generation stands at a crossroads — between the lessons of the past and the promise of the future. What we teach, tolerate, and pass on determines which road our children will walk. Today, that choice feels more urgent than ever.

In homes across America, parents are quietly waging the same battle our nation faces in public: how to raise children who are grounded in truth, self-respect, and moral conviction in a time that questions all three.

Two Generations, Two Americas

I have six children. My oldest son, Christopher (33), and my oldest daughter, Crystal (22), were born in a different time — before the world became as digital, divided, and distracted as it is now. They grew up with an America that still believed in showing up, not just logging in.

But I'll be honest — I wasn't always there the way I wanted to be— the way I should have been. I was young — didn't know any better. I was learning what manhood really meant. I didn't know I wasn't doing enough. I was very young at the beginning of that relationship and could blame it on my then wife who was four year my senior as being controlling but I see now that she was being strong where I was weak. But life has a way of teaching you that presence and consistency matter more than anything else.

Christopher and Crystal learned strength and independence on their own terms. They built their own understanding of family, of faith, of perseverance. We don't always share the same views or experiences, I hope with time a quiet understanding will become built between us — one built on respect, forgiveness, and understanding.

Then there's my younger four — the ones I am now raising deliberately and purposefully. Ameer (8) is thoughtful and curious, always full of questions that challenge me to think deeper. Khairi (5) has the kind of energy that reminds me how much joy can come from simple moments. Ny'Adia (2), my little girl, has already learned how to command attention with her smile and boldness looking exactly like Crystal. And baby Lateef (8 months) brings the kind of peace only a child's innocence can offer — a daily reminder that tomorrow is still worth fighting for.

They've never lived with their older siblings, and their worlds barely overlap. But that separation — between two generations under the same Woolen name — mirrors what's happening across America. Two worlds, both American, both good at heart, but shaped by completely different influences and realities.

Presence Over Policy

Raising my younger children has taught me something that every policymaker should understand: no law, no budget, no program can replace presence. I make it a point to be there — not just at meals or milestones, but in the quiet, ordinary moments. When I walk Ameer through his homework or watch his beautiful mother Latitia do it or when Khairi climbs into my lap to ask a question that's far too big for his age, I see the responsibility we all share to build clarity where confusion has crept in.

We live in an age where parents are being replaced by screens, and conviction is being replaced by convenience. We are raising children who can navigate a phone better than their own emotions. That's not progress — that's a warning.

If America wants to restore its foundation, it must start by restoring the presence of parents, the accountability of leaders, and the moral compass of communities. We can't outsource our values.

Education, Identity, and the Battle for Truth

Education is the cornerstone of every nation, and in many ways, it's also the battlefield of every generation. I want my children to learn how to think, not what to think. Schools should build intellect and character, not replace parental guidance with political or social agendas.

In Texas, the move toward school vouchers gives families a real voice in education. It gives parents like me — and many others — a choice. But choice means responsibility. Whether a child is in public school, private school, or charter school, what they learn at home will always matter most.

As a father, I believe that a child's sense of identity should come naturally — from their faith, their family, and their lived experience — not from social pressures or trends. Gender, self-

51

worth, and purpose are not classroom experiments; they are lifelong journeys shaped by truth, love, and understanding.

My children are growing up in a world where their innocence is constantly under attack — not always with malice, but with confusion. So, I make it my duty to talk with them, to listen to them, and to help them see that who they are is already enough.

Marriage, Family, and the Foundation of Stability

Marriage and family are not outdated institutions; they are the backbone of civilization. Civil unions have their place in law, but marriage — as a sacred covenant between a man and a woman — is what gives society its structure.

A home built on respect, faith, and shared values produces stability. And when the home weakens, the nation follows. I have seen both sides of that truth — the strength that comes from commitment and the struggle that comes from separation.

We must protect and promote family life, not as a political position, but as a moral imperative. America cannot afford to keep breaking its own foundation while hoping for balance.

The Generational Divide and the Path Forward

When I look at my children — the older two living their own lives and the younger four growing under my care — I see two sets of experiences that represent the same country. One set carries the lessons of what was; the other carries the hope of what can still be.

That divide is not something to regret — it's something to reconcile. America can do the same. The older generation carries wisdom, discipline, and tradition. The younger generation carries energy, innovation, and boldness. One without the other cannot survive.

The Crossroads of Character

The future of this nation depends on what kind of people we raise in our homes. Not just educated or ambitious — but honest, grounded, and morally firm.

When I sit with Ameer and Khairi at the counter, when I see Ny'Adia learning to talk, or hold Lateef in my arms, I think about the world they'll inherit. And I realize that everything we fight for — from education reform to moral clarity — must be built for them.

The fight isn't about power; it's about preparation. It's about making sure our children inherit not only opportunity, but direction.

Our families are microcosms of the nation. When we restore purpose in the home, we restore hope in the country. The next generation is watching how we lead, how we love, and how we live our convictions.

America's future — like my own family's future — depends on what we choose to pass on: confusion or clarity, distraction or direction, division or unity.

And I choose unity. I choose faith. I choose to raise my children — and help guide this country — with presence, truth, and unwavering purpose.

Reflection

Every home is a piece of the nation; every child, a reflection of its future. When we heal THE HOUSE, we heal the homeland.

PUN INTENDED!

— • —

Chapter 9 – The Presidency and the President: Power vs Purpose

Chapter 9 – The Presidency and the President: Power vs Purpose

There is a difference between holding power and being trusted with purpose. Somewhere along the way, America blurred the line between the two. We turned the presidency — once a sacred office of service — into a stage for performance. The office was meant to represent the people; now it often resembles a battleground for ego, celebrity, and party dominance.

But the presidency is not about personality. It is about responsibility — the burden of leading a free people without ever becoming their master.

The Office vs. The Occupant

The office of President is bigger than any one man or woman. It belongs to the people — not to a party, not to an ideology, not to a generation. Presidents come and go; the Constitution remains. Yet in the noise of modern politics, too many have begun to treat the office as a possession rather than a trust.

We have seen presidents who inspire unity and presidents who inflame division. We have witnessed leaders who elevated truth and those who weaponized it. And still, the weight of the office endures — because the presidency was designed to test character as much as competence.

A president should not seek applause but accountability. The true measure of leadership isn't in how loud the crowd cheers, but in how faithfully the leader serves when no one's watching.

The Theater of Power

Politics has become performance. The cameras, the tweets, the slogans — all of it designed to stir emotion more than reflection. But governing isn't entertainment. America doesn't need more showmen; it needs statesmen.

The presidency was never meant to be about personality cults. It was designed for balance — to keep ambition in check, to ensure that power remained in the hands of the governed. Yet, we've allowed our loyalty to personalities to overshadow our loyalty to principles.

When citizens begin to follow a person instead of a purpose, democracy starts to drift.

We can admire strong leadership without surrendering to it. We can respect authority without worshiping it. Because no matter who sits in the Oval Office, the people must remain the ultimate seat of power.

Presidency as Service

The best presidents in our history — Washington, Lincoln, Eisenhower, Kennedy, Reagan, Obama, and others — carried a deep understanding that the presidency was not theirs to keep. They understood it was a station of stewardship.

Each came from a different background, each carried different flaws and strengths, but all understood the same truth: *the presidency is temporary, but its impact is eternal.*

We must return to seeing the presidency as a sacred trust — not a throne. It is an office that demands humility, not hubris; empathy, not arrogance; vision, not vengeance.

The president's job is to unify, not to dominate. To speak for all, not just for some. To lift the nation's conscience higher than its conflicts.

The President We Need

America needs a president who listens before speaking, who leads without belittling, and who measures success not by polls but by progress.

We need a president who remembers that *"justice is blind,"* but leadership must not be deaf — deaf to the pain, fear, and hope of the people.

We need a president who governs from conviction, not convenience; one who understands that leadership is not control, but counsel.

A strong president does not fear criticism. A wise president welcomes it. Because democracy only thrives when truth is allowed to breathe.

The People's Role

We, the people, cannot keep blaming the office for what we elect into it. The presidency reflects us — our fears, our values, our maturity. If we choose spectacle, we will get chaos. If we choose substance, we will get stability.

The strength of the presidency is not determined by who sits in the chair, but by the character of the citizens who put them there.

That is why civic education, moral clarity, and honest conversation matter. The presidency begins long before Election Day. It begins in the hearts and homes of the people — in how we teach our children to lead, to disagree, and to serve.

When our homes produce character, our country produces leaders. When our homes produce confusion, our country produces chaos.

Restoring Purpose

The presidency must once again become the moral compass of the nation — not the megaphone of division.

It must remind us that the highest office in the land is not a reward, but a responsibility.

The goal is not to rule, but to represent; not to dominate, but to direct.

That is how we restore balance — when purpose outweighs power, and service replaces self-interest.

Reflection

The office of President belongs to the people; the man or woman who fills it is only its steward. When the seat forgets the soul, power becomes pride. True leadership is not about commanding attention — it's about earning trust.

— • —

Chapter 10 – Immigration: The Door and the Welcome

Chapter 10 – Immigration: The Door and the Welcome

America has always been a land of doors — some open, some closed, and some waiting to be rebuilt. The story of this nation began with movement: people leaving, seeking, and arriving. Every generation since has wrestled with the same question — *Who do we let in, and how do we remain ourselves while we do it?*

Immigration is not just a policy issue; it is a test of national character. It forces us to balance compassion with order, welcome with wisdom, and opportunity with obligation.

The Nation of the Door

A house without doors cannot protect what's inside. But a house whose doors never open cannot share its blessings. That balance is the moral core of immigration.

For centuries, America's doors have opened to those escaping war, persecution, or poverty — and in doing so, this nation has renewed its strength through the very diversity it once feared. Yet every open door also carries responsibility: for both the one entering and the one welcoming.

There is nothing racist about borders; they are the walls that define the house. The question is not whether America should have borders, but whether they serve justice and humanity at the same time.

Our immigration system must be *productive*, not *counterproductive* — one that honors the rule of law while recognizing the dignity of every person who seeks a better life.

Compassion and Order

Too often, compassion is used as a weapon, and order is used as a wall. The truth is, America needs both.

We can be compassionate toward those who flee danger, and still expect them to follow due process. We can enforce our laws firmly, and still treat people humanely. This is not contradiction — it is balance.

A chaotic border benefits no one. It overwhelms communities, burdens resources, and creates conditions where both citizens and migrants suffer. At the same time, cruelty toward those who seek safety dishonors our national creed.

The challenge is not choosing between heart and law — it is learning how to apply both with wisdom.

The Role of Responsibility

Every immigrant who enters America should understand not just their rights, but their responsibilities. Citizenship — whether earned by birth or by effort — carries the same duty: to respect the law, contribute to society, and defend the values that make freedom possible.

I believe in a path to citizenship for those who have lived, worked, and served here honorably. But that path must be lawful, structured, and rooted in merit — not political gamesmanship or emotional exploitation.

America should never close its doors to dreamers, but it must ensure those dreams don't come at the expense of fairness. Those who wait, apply, and follow the law deserve the same respect as those who arrive with hope.

We must build a system where compassion doesn't mean chaos — where the door opens wide enough for opportunity, but strong enough to protect the home.

The Economics of Immigration

Immigration is not just about borders; it's about balance. It affects wages, education, housing, healthcare, and national security. We need to stop treating it like a side issue — it's a cornerstone issue.

Illegal immigration often hurts the very people it claims to help — driving down wages, creating unsafe labor conditions, and straining local economies. Meanwhile, lawful immigration done right can enrich industries, strengthen communities, and renew innovation.

We must stop rewarding systems that encourage dependency or deception, and instead reward those who contribute, create, and commit to the American dream through honest effort.

A fair immigration policy doesn't just protect America's jobs — it preserves America's integrity.

The Human Story

Every immigrant carries a story — and every story deserves to be heard with dignity. But not every story means a right to entry. The challenge of leadership is to listen with empathy, but decide with clarity.

I've spoken to immigrants who built their lives from nothing — who opened small businesses, raised children who became doctors, teachers, and soldiers. I've also seen the heartbreak of families separated, of lives caught between nations and laws.

Both sides of that story are real, and both deserve our attention. The solution lies not in extremes, but in equilibrium — protecting borders while protecting humanity.

America's Identity

If America loses control of her borders, she loses part of her identity. But if she loses her compassion, she loses her soul.

The door must remain — strong, standing, and open to those who seek to enter with respect for the house they are joining. We are not just a land of immigrants; we are a land of laws. One gives us life, the other gives us order. Together, they give us peace.

Ask Us About Us – RC "Majid" Woolen Jr.

The question before us now is not whether we can fix immigration — but whether we can fix our will. Because policy without purpose is paper. Purpose requires courage.

Reflection

A house without a door cannot protect, but a door that never opens cannot welcome. America must do both — guard her walls and guide her guests. Mercy and order are not enemies; they are the hinges on which justice swings.

— • —

Chapter 11 – The Economy of Dignity

Chapter 11 – The Economy of Dignity

A nation's true wealth is not its currency — it is the character of the people who earn it.

For too long, our economic debates have focused on profit margins and policy points, while ignoring the one thing that makes any system work: the dignity of honest labor.

An economy without dignity becomes a machine.

An economy with dignity becomes a community.

Work and Worth

Work is not punishment — it is purpose. From the first farmer tilling the land to the factory worker clocking in before sunrise, America was built on the principle that effort brings elevation.

But somewhere along the way, work lost its respect.

We turned "jobs" into statistics instead of callings.

We started rewarding speculation more than service, and loopholes more than labor.

When a man or woman works hard and still can't afford to live decently, something is wrong — not just with the market, but with our moral compass.

We need an economy that restores *dignity to the doer*, not just dividends to the dealer.

The Forgotten Worker

Every generation has a group that gets left behind when technology, trade, or politics shift. The factory worker replaced by automation. The small business crushed by corporate consolidation. The family farmer priced out by global policy.

These aren't just "economic casualties" — they're Americans.

And when we let them fall, we weaken the moral spine of our nation.

We must fight for an economy that includes them again — that gives them tools, training, and trust to rebuild their futures.

No man should feel like his work doesn't matter.

No woman should feel like her labor is invisible.

No community should feel abandoned because it isn't trendy or profitable.

Small Business, Big Heart

The small business is America's truest economic engine.

It represents courage, creativity, and commitment — the courage to risk, the creativity to solve, and the commitment to serve.

But today, that spirit is being smothered by regulations written for corporations and taxes that punish independence.

We must simplify, not strangle. We must encourage, not encumber.

If we want strong communities, we must protect the people who *build* them — not the ones who buy them out.

Every barber shop, mechanic's garage, daycare, restaurant, or home-based business is a statement of faith in the American dream. Government's job should be to fuel that dream — not frustrate it.

Economic Independence

Economic freedom is political freedom.

If a man depends on a system that controls his income, that system controls his voice. That's why dependency — whether through excessive welfare or corporate greed — is dangerous to democracy.

The goal of government should not be to *feed* people, but to *free* them — to equip them with opportunity, not trap them in obligation.

When work is available, wages are fair, and taxes are reasonable, dignity flourishes naturally.

I believe in a system where every able citizen can rise through discipline, education, and enterprise — not entitlement.

The Family and the Future

A strong economy starts at the dinner table.

When parents have stable work, families have stable lives. When fathers are active, children learn the value of effort. When mothers are respected, society grows healthy.

Family stability isn't just a moral issue — it's an economic one.

Broken homes lead to broken focus. A culture that devalues family will always pay the price in productivity, discipline, and peace.

That's why policies that strengthen families — tax relief for parents, affordable childcare, support for home ownership — are not "social programs." They're *national investments*.

Faith, Frugality, and the Future

I look around and can see that wealth without wisdom is a curse, and comfort without character is corruption.

We must bring conscience back into capitalism.

Every dollar earned honestly should bless more than the hand that holds it — it should uplift the home, the neighborhood, and the next generation.

We can have prosperity *with principle*.

We can have growth *with gratitude*.

We can build wealth that honors God, country, and community — not greed.

The truest wealth is not what's in the wallet, but what's in the work.

When a man's labor feeds his family and lifts his spirit, that's the economy of dignity.

— • —

Chapter 12 – Faith and the Freedom to Believe

Chapter 12 – Faith and the Freedom to Believe

Faith is the heartbeat of a people. It shapes their hope, their habits, and their understanding of right and wrong.

Remove faith from the soul of a nation, and that nation becomes mechanical — powerful maybe, but hollow at its core.

America was never meant to be hollow.

It was meant to be *whole* — a union of believers, thinkers, and seekers who trusted that moral conviction and freedom could exist side by side.

We are not just a nation of laws; we are a nation of values.

And those values — honesty, compassion, responsibility, humility — come from something higher than politics.

Faith as Foundation

The founders may not have agreed on every doctrine, but they understood one thing clearly: liberty comes from the Creator, not from the government.

That's why the Constitution protects the *free exercise* of religion — not the government's permission to practice it.

Faith keeps power in check. It reminds men in high offices that there is an authority above them.

It tells the rich that their riches will be measured by how they use them, and the strong that their strength is a trust, not a weapon.

When we silence faith in the public square, we invite arrogance into it. And arrogance — the belief that man alone can define truth — is the oldest lie ever told.

Faith Beyond Labels

I am an African American

I am a Native American.

I am a Muslim American.

But the common ground that we all stand on is that we all are Americans. I believe that God made us different so that we might learn to understand one another.

Faith is not meant to divide — it is meant to define the best within each of us.

We may worship differently, but we all kneel before the same reality: that life itself is sacred, and that no man gives or takes it without accountability.

The Christian, the Muslim, the Jew, the believer and the doubter — all deserve the same protection to think, to speak, and to worship freely.

That is what separates us from nations built on fear or forced ideology.

Faith is freedom's first friend.

Morality and Modern Confusion

Today, our children are growing up in a fog of moral confusion.

They are told to question everything except their own questioning. They are taught tolerance for everything except truth itself.

Schools once partnered with parents to raise good citizens; now too many systems seem determined to raise confused ones.

Faith used to be seen as strength — now it's branded as "controversial."

We are not just facing a culture war. We are facing a *value collapse*.

And rebuilding those values means reintroducing accountability — to something, or someone, greater than ourselves.

Faith does not mean forcing religion on others. It means refusing to be forced *away* from it.

Faith and Governance

A faithful leader doesn't have to preach — but he must have principles.

He must understand that justice without mercy becomes tyranny, and liberty without restraint becomes chaos.

When I talk about bringing faith back into public life, I'm not talking about religion in government — I'm talking about *conscience in leadership*.

A conscience that says: I can't buy votes with lies.

I can't trade truth for power.

And I can't forget the people who trusted me to represent them honestly.

A Congress guided by conscience is stronger than one guided by polls.

Unity Through Understanding

Faith gives us a way to connect across differences.

When we share what we believe — not to convert, but to converse — we build bridges that politics cannot burn.

In Texas, I've met Christians who taught me humility, Jews who taught me discipline, atheists who taught me courage, and Muslims who taught me patience.

That's America — a quilt of conviction stitched together by respect.

We do not have to agree on *everything* to stand for *something*.

Teach your children that faith is not a costume to wear on holy days, but a compass to carry every day. It will not make life easier — it will make it clearer.

— • —

Chapter 13 The Moral Question: Policy and Principle

Chapter 13 – The Moral Question: Policy and Principle

There are moments in a nation's life when laws and leadership can no longer be measured only by what is legal — but by what is *right*. We are living in one of those moments.

When policy loses its moral compass, government becomes little more than machinery without a soul. That is what we are witnessing today — a Congress that debates endlessly but stands for little; a society that argues about everything but agrees on almost nothing.

That's why I am running — not to take a side, but to **redefine what it means to take a stand**.

Civil Union and Marriage — *Somewhat* Equal, Yet Not the Same

There are truths that must be faced without fear.

Marriage is not a man-made invention; it is a natural and spiritual bond. It is the root of family, the bedrock of community, the beginning of moral order. But civil union, while legal, is an arrangement — it recognizes companionship, not covenant.

Both have rights. Both have meaning. But they are not the same.

When government began to blur that line, it didn't just change policy — it changed the moral language of the country. The question now is not about denying anyone's dignity; it's about **protecting the foundation of society**.

Those who choose a civil union should be afforded legal rights of *partnership*. But **the word marriage carries a sacred charge** — one that belongs not to the government, but to the divine. It is not hate to protect that distinction; it is honesty.

We cannot allow political correctness to rewrite the natural laws of creation.

The Fight for Our Children

If there is one thing that keeps me up at night, it's not inflation, or foreign policy, or even the budget battles in Washington — it's our children.

We are confusing their minds before we can shape their character. We are teaching them to *choose* an identity before they even know what identity means.

A child's journey of self-discovery should be guided, not manipulated. We must return to the understanding that **gender is not an opinion — it's a creation**.

As a father of six, I have seen two generations rise under two very different skies. My older children, Christopher and Crystal, grew up in a world where right and wrong still had boundaries. My younger children — Ameer, Khairi, Ny'Adia, and Lateef — are being raised in a world where those boundaries are being erased in the name of "freedom."

True freedom must be rooted in truth. When we allow ideology to replace nature, we are not liberating children — we are **leading them into confusion**.

And what's worse — we are forcing taxpayers to finance it.

No government has the right to take your hard-earned money and use it to underwrite surgeries or procedures that deny nature itself. That is not compassion; that is coercion.

Our children need guidance, not government-funded confusion.

Education: Building Minds, Not Machines

Education is the cornerstone of every great civilization. But in America, the classroom has become a battlefield.

Texas has begun experimenting with vouchers and school choice, and I believe this movement, if guided correctly, could be one of the most transformative ideas of our generation.

When parents are given the freedom to choose, they become partners in education — not prisoners of bureaucracy. Charter schools, private schools, home schools — all should have the ability to shape their curriculum according to their values and vision.

However, with freedom comes responsibility. We must ensure that **education remains a place of truth, not indoctrination**. Let science be science, faith be faith, and values be taught not as commands, but as compass points.

We must remind this nation that education should *enlighten*, not *engineer*.

The President and the Presidency

In recent years, we've confused the person with the position.

We have learned to idolize or demonize individuals while neglecting the sacred structure of the presidency itself.

The President is a man or woman; the Presidency is an institution. One will pass, the other must endure.

When I speak of strengthening Congress, I mean restoring that sacred balance — where each branch respects the other, and the American people respect them both.

Our founders never intended for one personality to dominate the Republic. They intended for leadership to be humble enough to serve, wise enough to listen, and brave enough to act — even when it's unpopular.

The office must be respected again, but so must the people who give it power.

Immigration: A System of Order, Not Disorder

America has always been a nation of immigrants — but it must also be a nation of laws.

We cannot continue to build a future on a system that rewards the disorderly and punishes the obedient. Immigration reform is not about closing doors; it's about **fixing the hinges**.

A productive immigration policy is one that prioritizes contribution over chaos. If you come here seeking to work, to learn, to contribute — you are welcome. But if you come to exploit or evade, then this land must draw a line.

It's time to modernize our system, streamline legal entry, and hold accountable those who exploit human suffering for political gain.

We need compassion, but we also need control. A border without balance is not mercy — it is madness.

Restoring Trust in Congress

If there is one institution that should stand as the moral backbone of our democracy, it's Congress. But today, it feels more like a fractured spine — bent under the weight of money, party loyalty, and pride.

Ask Us About Us – RC "Majid" Woolen Jr.

We've watched leaders take oaths to the people, then bow to the pressure of their party. We've watched legislation become less about the common good and more about scoring political points. And the American people — hardworking, God-fearing, and loyal — are left feeling betrayed.

The people's trust has been broken not by our democracy, but by the dysfunction within its walls.

I'm not running to join a team.

I'm running to **restore the table** where both sides can sit again, look each other in the eye, and speak for the people who sent them there.

It's time for a Congress that listens more than it lectures. A Congress that works for solutions, not slogans.

A Congress that remembers: it is the servant of the people — not their master.

We cannot mend the garment of America if the very hands meant to sew it are too busy pointing fingers.

So I stand as an Independent, not because I reject both parties, but because I refuse to be owned by either. I will work with anyone who works for America — and I will stand against anyone who works against her, no matter their party or power.

This is not rebellion. This is **renewal**.

Ask Us About Us – RC "Majid" Woolen Jr.

The same way a father must regain his family's trust through action, not excuses — Congress must regain the trust of the people through courage, not campaigns.

And that is why I am running:

To strengthen Congress.

To restore its honor.

To remind America that principle is still powerful, and that truth still stands taller than politics. "Truth smashes the brains out of falsehood."

When I look at the chambers of Congress, I see a reflection of the American household — voices talking over one another, emotions high, tempers quick. But wisdom does not shout to be heard. It speaks to bring peace, and when wisdom speaks truth, peace eventually follows.

If we want to heal this nation, we must first steady its voice.

Let that voice come from conscience, not party lines.

Let it speak truth to power, and kindness to the people.

Let it sound like America again.

Reflection

When I look at my children, I see the America I am fighting for — one that still believes in truth, order, and freedom.

*If one day, my sons will ask me what I stood for when the world started to blur the lines between right and wrong. I want to tell them: **I stood for principle. I stood for them.***

Every law I support, every policy I propose, is rooted in one simple conviction: That a nation without moral courage cannot lead the world, and a Congress without conscience cannot serve the people.

*I'm not running to play politics. I'm running to **raise the standard**.*

— • —

Chapter 14 – The Great American Costume Party

Chapter 14 – The Great American Costume Party

There's a show running in Washington, and everyone seems to have forgotten it's supposed to be government.

The stage lights are bright, the cameras are rolling, and the cast is enormous. One side dresses in blue, the other in red. Both promise a brand-new act every election season, yet the script never changes. The audience keeps paying for tickets anyway—taxes, inflation, frustration—just to watch the same play performed with different costumes.

The set never moves, the lines never evolve, and the people in the cheap seats keep wondering when the story will finally turn in their favor. But it never does, because this isn't a republic anymore—it's repertory theatre.

The Performance

The Left and Right are rival troupes competing for applause, not truth. They act like enemies on stage, then toast each other backstage. The media runs concessions, selling outrage in paper cups. Lobbyists write the dialogue. And the extras—those of us who still believe in work, prayer, and family—are told to sit quietly while the "stars" monologue about representation.

Costumes change, masks switch, but the performance remains. It's easier to play roles than to solve problems. And while they debate which color owns the curtain, the roof over the stage leaks, the foundation cracks, and the audience grows restless.

The Cost of the Show

This theater feeds on division; unity doesn't sell tickets. The audience is trained to boo on cue. They don't see the wires pulling at their emotions, the cue cards flashing anger or fear. The longer the people argue about the actors, the less they notice the building is burning.

Meanwhile, the children—our future critics—sit in the balcony watching adults behave like caricatures. They see the shouting, the finger-pointing, the blame, and they start to believe that performance is leadership. I refuse to let my children inherit that illusion. They will learn that character is built off-stage, not performed for cameras.

The Audience Is Waking Up

Every show runs out of magic eventually. The spotlights start to flicker. The applause gets thin. People begin to whisper, "Is anyone actually running this place?" You can feel it in every diner, every church parking lot, every online forum that hasn't lost its soul yet. Americans are tired of actors. They want authenticity again.

Both parties sense it but are too addicted to the applause to stop. They fear silence more than failure. But silence is coming—the kind that follows when an audience stands up and walks out.

Independent: Un-Owned, Un-Scripted, Un-Bought

That's where I enter—not to audition, but to end the play. I'm not here to steal anyone's role; I'm here to close the curtain and rebuild the stage. I run as an Independent because independence is not isolation—it's integrity. It's the courage to govern without a teleprompter, to speak truth without checking the party memo.

Both sides ask, "Who's your director?" I answer, "The people." They ask, "Who funds your show?" I answer, "The audience I serve."

Representation isn't performance—it's presence. It means showing up when the lights are off, when the cameras are gone, and the work still needs doing. That's what this campaign stands for.

Ask Us About Us: A Campaign for Correct Representation

That phrase isn't a slogan; it's a declaration. Ask Us About Us means: stop guessing who we are. Stop letting pollsters and pundits narrate our lives. We don't need new costumes—we need honest conversation.

A Campaign for Correct Representation means: leaders who actually reflect the people's values, not the parties' demands. And Come to Common Ground is the invitation: to leave the balcony, step onto the same floor, and talk like citizens again.

Because this government doesn't need better actors—it needs adults.

The Curtain Call

When the lights go down on this old production, the audience will still be here, standing in the dark, waiting for truth. That's when a new act begins—not of performance, but of principle. No costumes. No scripts. No applause. Just service.

That's what I'm running for. Not a seat in the theatre, but a place in the workshop—where the real rebuilding begins.

Ask Us About Us — A Campaign for Correct Representation. Come to Common Ground.

When I tuck my children in at night, I don't want them to inherit a world of performances. I want them to inherit a country of principles. I tell them that truth isn't always loud, but it is always strong. I teach them that real leadership isn't about applause; it's about accountability.

— • —

Chapter 15 – Restoring the Republic: Standing on Common Ground

Chapter 15 – Restoring the Republic: Standing on Common Ground

There's a rip in the garment of America.

Some say it began with politics, others say with culture — but however it started, it's growing wider every year.

The left blames the right. The right blames the left.

And in between them, the people — *the real America* — are being stretched thin.

I'm not running to take a side.

I'm running to bring a balance.

I'm running to strengthen the Congress — not for one party's victory, but for *the people's recovery.*

The Middle Ground Is Not Weak Ground

Somewhere along the line, we started to confuse moderation with weakness.

We began to think that if you stood in the middle, you stood for nothing.

But that's wrong.

The middle is not where the uncertain stand — it's where the *builders* stand.

It's the place where you can reach both sides with both hands, pulling them closer, mending the tear that threatens to pull the nation apart.

We don't need more partisans in Congress.

We need more *patriots* — men and women willing to see beyond red and blue and stand firmly in red, white, and blue.

That's why I'm running as an Independent.

Not because I don't see value in the parties, but because I see value in the people — and they've been left out of the conversation for far too long.

Mending the Garment

A divided Congress can't serve a united country.

When the fabric of government is torn, the people feel the draft.

Every issue — from education to healthcare to immigration — gets tangled in party labels before it ever reaches honest debate.

Each vote becomes a battle for political ground instead of common ground.

I'm not here to tear down the parties. I'm here to sew them back together — stitch by stitch, law by law, with respect, reason, and responsibility.

We don't need to agree on everything, but we must agree on *something*:

that the people's business should never be held hostage by political games.

When Democrats and Republicans speak, I listen to both.

Because I know that truth isn't owned by either — it's revealed through dialogue between both.

A Congress of Conscience

Congress was meant to be the people's chamber — not a battlefield, not a brand.

But look at it now:

Members vote not on principle, but on party.

Debates end before they begin.

And the American people are left wondering, "Who's representing *us*?"

An Independent voice can change that.

Because independence means obligation — not to party, but to principle.

It means you can speak truth without asking permission.

You can cross the aisle without crossing your conscience.

That's what I intend to do.

Not to weaken Congress, but to strengthen it — to remind every member that their seat belongs to the people, not to the platform.

The Strength of a Bridge

I come to believe that a bridge is stronger than a wall.

A wall divides — but a bridge holds weight from both sides.

And the stronger the tension, the stronger the bridge must be.

That's what this moment requires — men and women willing to *hold the tension* of our time and not run from it.

To stand between disagreement and despair and say, "We can fix this — together."

My goal isn't to silence Democrats or Republicans — it's to give both a reason to listen again.

Because without communication, there can be no cooperation.

And without cooperation, Congress cannot function.

Why I'm Running

I'm running because I believe America can still heal.

I'm running because our children deserve to inherit a country that debates ideas, not identities.

I'm running because silence has become complicity — and I refuse to be silent.

I'm running as an Independent because independence is where solutions live.

It's where you can honor conservative values without abandoning compassion.

It's where you can respect progress without rejecting principle.

It's where America was always meant to stand — not in extremes, but in *equilibrium*.

We've spent decades tearing at the fabric of our democracy.

It's time to start *mending* it.

When something is broken, don't throw it away — fix it.

The same goes for this country.

Don't run from the mess. Stand in it. Work through it.

That's how families heal. That's how nations endure.

— • —

Epilogue – Rise, Stand, and Mend

Rise, Stand, and Mend
The Mending of a Nation

There is a moment in every nation's story when it must decide whether it will rise to its calling or collapse under its contradictions. America is at that moment now. Our divisions are no longer intellectual disagreements — they are emotional fractures, cultural wounds, spiritual breaks, and political addictions. The garment has torn, and the threads are snapping fast.

We have been warned by history many times. Great nations do not fall because of an enemy at the gate — they fall when their people stop believing in each other, when trust dies, when truth weakens, when citizens choose party over principle and power over purpose. Rome fell this way. Empires fell this way. And if we are not vigilant, America could stumble down that same road.

But I still believe this nation can be mended. I believe the fabric can be repaired. I believe there is more strength in our common ground than in our weaponized differences. I believe we are still a people capable of greatness — not the empty, slogan kind of greatness, but the humble, sacrificial, disciplined kind that builds generations.

That is the America I see:

An America where Congress serves the people and not the parties.

An America where children are protected, families are strengthened, and faith is not ridiculed but respected.

An America that stands firm on law, borders, and responsibility — yet still extends mercy, compassion, and opportunity to those who seek a better life the right way.

An America that argues, debates, and disagrees — but does not hate, cancel, or destroy.

An America where conservative and liberal are not enemies, but balances — like left and right steps in a single forward march.

If we choose it, we can write a new chapter for this country — one stitched together by truth, honor, family, and common ground. But understand this: **the time for spectatorship is over**. A republic cannot be saved from the couch, the sidelines, or the comment section. It must be saved by citizens — by *We the People*.

So I am stepping into the arena — not as a partisan soldier, not as a professional politician, but as a man who refuses to let America tear itself apart. I am running as an Independent because I refuse to be owned by either machine. I choose to serve the people, not the party. And I ask you to stand with me — not on the left, not on the right, but on the solid ground of principle, accountability, and American identity.

This is our warning.

This is our vision.

Now here is our charge:

Stand. Speak. Act. Come to common ground and fight for a Congress that represents the people. Ask Us About Us — a campaign for correct representation.

RC "Majid" Woolen Jr.
Independent, Texas Congressional District 24

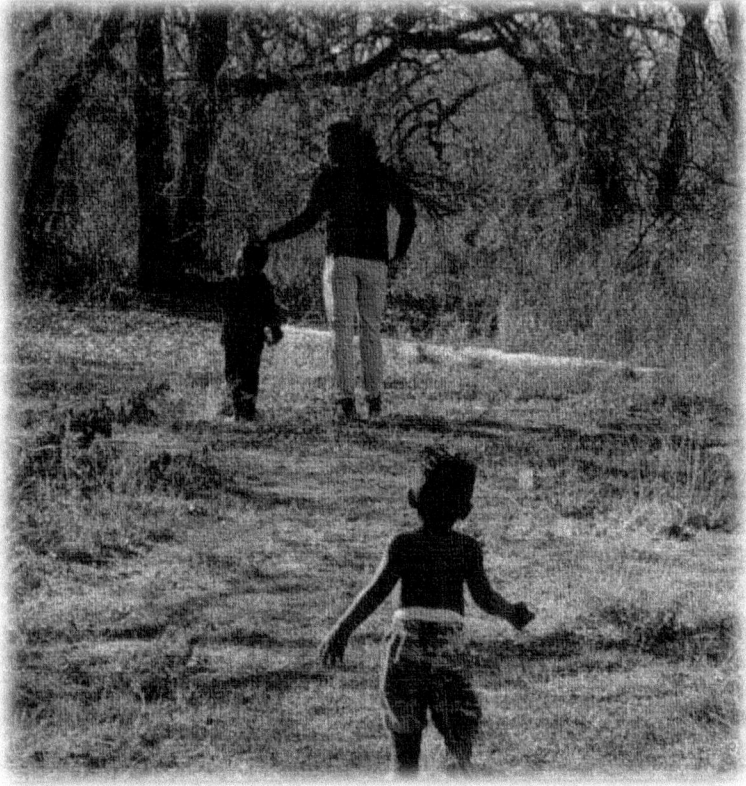

BACK COVER

We've argued long enough. Now it's time to understand each other.

Before America can heal, it must listen. Before we rise, we must understand.

In *Ask Us About Us: A Campaign for Correct Representation — Come to Common Ground*, RC "Majid" Woolen Jr. calls on Americans to rise above division and rediscover the values that unite us. Blending personal reflection with moral conviction, he challenges both parties — and every citizen — to lead with integrity, listen with empathy, and act with accountability.

Part memoir and part manifesto, *Ask Us About Us* speaks from faith, culture, and conscience. It is a reminder that the strength of this nation lies not in its arguments, but in its courage to mend what has been torn and stand together on common ground.

"Unity is not compromise—it's strength."

A MEInc Publication
Majid Enterprises,
Inc. 3540 E. Broad
St 120-408
Mansfield, TX
76063-5633
www.MajidEnterpri
sesInc.com
www.AskUsAbout
Us.com

Ask Us About Us – RC "Majid" Woolen Jr.

ISBN 979-8-218-94342-4

9 798218 943424 >

www.ingramcontent.com/pod-product-compliance
Lightning Source LLC
Chambersburg PA
CBHW070929270326
41927CB00011B/2786